PUPPY

TRAINING TECHNIQUES

Essential Commands for a Well-Behaved Puppy

ALICE C. STONE

All rights reserved. No part of this publication may be reproduced, distributed, or transmitted in any form or by any means, including photocopying, recording, or other electronic or mechanical methods, without the prior written permission of the publisher, except in the case of brief quotations embodied in critical reviews and certain other noncommercial uses permitted by copyright law. For permission requests, write to the publisher, addressed "Attention: Permissions Coordinator," at the address below.

Copyright © 2024 by Alice C. Stone

Table of Content

INTRODUCTION 7

CHAPTER 1: GETTING STARTED WITH PUPPY TRAINING 9

    Teach With Words 12

    Avoid Treat-Based Training 13

    Establishing Respect 13

    Crate Training 14

    Acceptance 15

    Household Rules 16

CHAPTER 2: HOW DOES A PUPPY THINK? 18

    Staring 20

    Looking Sad 20

    Barking Repeatedly 21

    Cocking Their Head 21

CHAPTER 3: BENEFITS OF CRATE TRAINING 22

    Helps in Housebreaking 24

    Hinders Destructive Chewing 25

    Keeps Your Dog Safe 25

Prevents the Formation of Problem Behaviors 25

Safety and Security 26

Addressing Behavioral Problems 26

Calming Your Puppy 26

Safe Travel 27

CHAPTER 4: CRATE TRAINING BASICS ... 28

Introducing The Crate 29

Crate Training Safety 30

CHAPTER 5: HOW TO TEACH YOUR PUPPY ROUTINES 32

House Rules 33

Potty Routine 34

Meal Schedule 34

Exercise Routine 35

CHAPTER 6: THE 5 ESSENTIAL COMMANDS TO TEACH YOUR PUPPY 36

Teaching Your Puppy to Sit 37

Teaching the Command "Stay" 38

Teaching Your Puppy to Lie Down 39

Teaching Recall 40

Teaching Your Dog to Heel 41

Training Tips 42

CHAPTER 7: HOUSEBREAKING YOUR PUPPY IN 4 EASY STEPS 43

    Have Patience 44

    When to Start Housebreaking 45

    Create a Schedule 45

    Using a Crate 46

CHAPTER 8: HOW TO CORRECT BAD BEHAVIOR 47

    Dogs Need Rules 48

    Training Your Puppy 48

    Stop Your Dog From Biting and Chewing . 49

    Stop Jumping 50

    Stopping Rough Play 50

    Stopping Begging 51

    Managing Excessive Barking 51

    Addressing Digging 52

    Seeking Professional Help 52

CHAPTER 9: FINAL TIPS FOR TRAINING YOUR PUPPY 53

    Listen to Your Puppy 55

    Show Plenty of Affection 55

Welcome, adorable fluffball

Consider Your Puppy's Preferences 56
Give Clear Instructions 56
Maintain Consistency 56
Set Realistic Expectations 57
Provide a Proper Diet 57
Use Reinforcement Wisely 58
Bribery Doesn't Work 58
Granting Freedom Gradually 59
CHAPTER 10: NEXT-LEVEL TRAINING 60
Building on Basic Commands 60
Advanced Tricks and Skills 61
Impulse Control and Focus 62
Socialization and Public Etiquette 63
Continued Learning and Challenges 64
CONCLUSION 65

INTRODUCTION

Welcoming a new dog into your life is one of the most thrilling experiences, especially when it's a puppy! Puppies have a way of charming everyone they meet. Holding a puppy is a joy that few can resist. However, they can also be quite mischievous. Like children, they need guidance and boundaries. They naturally exhibit puppy behaviors, and it's your role to guide them in growing into well-behaved dogs.

The effort is well worth it, as dogs offer so much in return. They teach us invaluable lessons, such as:

- Living in the present
- Loving unconditionally

Welcome, adorable fluffball

- Forgiving easily
- Being non-judgmental

That said, bringing a dog into your home comes with its own set of challenges. Training is crucial for a harmonious life together. But rest assured, you're not alone in this journey! This guide is designed to help you transform your puppy into a well-mannered dog.

"Puppy Training Techniques" is packed with practical advice and straightforward guidance. Here's a glimpse of what you'll find:

- Understanding your puppy's behavior and body language
- The benefits of crate training and how to implement it
- Teaching the essential commands: "Sit," "Stay," "Lie Down," "Come," and "Heel"
- Housebreaking techniques
- Correcting unwanted behaviors like biting, jumping, and excessive barking
- Plus, many more tips and strategies for successful puppy raising

A well-trained puppy is a joy to be around. Let's explore how to achieve that together. Ready to start? Let's go!

Welcome, adorable fluffball

CHAPTER 1: GETTING STARTED WITH PUPPY TRAINING

"Training a puppy is like raising a child. Every single interaction is a training opportunity."

Key Point: Puppy training is about teaching your puppy to follow your guidance. It's essential to know what, when, and how to teach your puppy.

10 | *Welcome, adorable fluffball*

Training begins the moment you bring your puppy home. Your responses to your puppy's actions are crucial, as they can either reinforce good behavior or lead to unwanted habits. While having a puppy is delightful, it can also be challenging. Puppies are curious and joyful, but they require guidance and patience. Being prepared to handle the challenges of puppy training will make the process smoother and less stressful.

Establishing routines is key to helping your puppy feel secure. For example, always placing food and water bowls in the same location helps build consistency. You should establish and teach your puppy:

- A daily schedule
- The location of the food bowl
- Feeding times
- The designated sleeping area and bedtime
- Wake-up times
- Bathroom routines
- Walk and play times

How you teach these routines matters. Using the right training methods will help your puppy learn effectively and be well-adjusted. If not approached correctly, your puppy may develop undesirable behaviors and try to assert control over the household. It's important that you guide your puppy's learning and not the other way around.

Teach With Words

After your puppy has learned the two essential words, you can introduce additional vocabulary. The two key words to start with are:

- 'NO'
- 'GOOD'

Training isn't just about establishing routines; it also involves teaching your puppy specific words. When your puppy behaves well, praise them with "good," and when they do something undesirable, use "no." You can start this training when your puppy is around two months old. The way you teach these words is crucial; your body language and tone significantly impact how your puppy understands these commands. If your puppy is older than three months when you bring them home, begin teaching these words immediately.

Avoid Treat-Based Training

While puppies love treats, it's best to avoid using them as the primary tool for training. You might wonder why this is discouraged. Relying on treats can give your puppy too much control, making them decide whether to obey based on their hunger. This approach can lead to a misunderstanding that they only need to listen when a treat is offered.

This doesn't mean you should avoid treats entirely. They can be used as rewards, especially when teaching tricks, but shouldn't be the main method of training. Regularly coaxing your puppy with treats can undermine effective training.

Establishing Respect

Your puppy will only listen to you if they respect you. It's important for your puppy to understand that you are the leader in the home. Without respect, your puppy might know the words and routines but choose not to obey. A lack of respect often stems from inconsistent training or excessive pampering. It's crucial to consistently assert your role as the leader.

Respect training is about more than just knowing the words you want your puppy to learn; it's about how you teach them.

Your puppy should be eager to follow your instructions, understanding that you are in charge.

Crate Training

You can begin crate training when your puppy is around two to three months old. A crate helps protect your puppy from household accidents and is an essential tool for housebreaking. Think of the crate as your puppy's personal space, not as a confinement. Initially, your puppy might resist being in the crate, but over time, they will see it as a safe space to rest and retreat from household activities.

For a new puppy, the crate serves as both a training tool and a sleeping area. Once accustomed to the crate, it also makes it easier to transport your puppy, whether to the vet or during travel.

Housebreaking

Start housebreaking when your puppy is two to three months old. At this age, puppies, especially small breeds, have very limited control over their bladders, similar to an infant. It's crucial to begin housebreaking as soon as you bring your puppy home to establish a routine. This early training helps prevent accidents in the house, which can become a difficult habit to break if not addressed promptly.

Create a consistent schedule for bathroom breaks to encourage cooperation. There are various methods to housebreak your puppy, such as using a crate, a doggy door, or even a litter box for smaller breeds. You'll find more detailed guidance on this in Chapter 7 - Housebreaking Your Puppy in 4 Easy Steps.

Acceptance

Handling your puppy is essential for them to accept grooming and care routines, such as brushing, bathing, nail clipping, wearing a collar or harness, and taking medication. It's important for your puppy to see you as the leader in these situations. This isn't just about setting boundaries but also about teaching respect. Incorporate respect training alongside vocabulary lessons to help your puppy understand and accept these necessary routines.

Gentleness

Teaching your puppy to be gentle is crucial. They should learn not to nip or chew on people's hands or feet. This training usually starts with the mother dog, who corrects her puppies during play. Your role is to continue this training by setting clear limits on what is acceptable behavior. This involves not just caring for your puppy but also correcting them when they start to exhibit undesirable behaviors. Remember, you set the boundaries for what is considered good and bad behavior.

Household Rules

It's important to establish clear household rules for your puppy. Decide what behaviors are acceptable and which are not. For example, chewing on shoes, jumping on people, sitting on furniture, entering the kitchen during cooking, taking socks from the laundry, sleeping in your bed, or barking at strangers from the window. Everyone in the household should be consistent in enforcing these rules to avoid confusing your puppy. Consistency is key in helping your puppy understand what is expected of them.

Tips for Older Puppies

The training schedule for an older puppy is not fundamentally different from that of a younger one. Regardless of age, the training process should begin with basic vocabulary training. This includes establishing a routine, using praise and corrective words, crate training, teaching acceptance, encouraging gentleness, and setting household rules. If your older puppy is still eating from your hand, barking at strangers, or not responding to commands, now is the time to begin basic training.

Start with simple, essential commands like "no" and "good" before progressing to commands like "stay," "sit," or "heel." Respect is foundational, no matter your puppy's age. Once your puppy understands these basic commands, you can move on to more complex instructions, such as walking calmly on a leash, coming when called, lying down or staying still, waiting at an open door, and stopping barking on command. These skills require your puppy to learn not just the words but also the actions associated with them. It's important to teach these words and behaviors in a consistent and clear manner, reinforcing your role as the leader. Avoid using treats as the sole means of training.

Leadership in training does not involve harsh methods like hitting or using choke collars. It involves subtle cues and actions during interactions with your puppy. Puppies will misbehave occasionally, and your response is crucial. Consistently responding inappropriately can lead to continued misbehavior, while responding appropriately helps establish you as the leader. It's beneficial to start this training as early as possible, as it allows you to instill good habits and correct undesirable behaviors from the beginning.

Welcome, adorable fluffball

CHAPTER 2: HOW DOES A PUPPY THINK?

"There is no psychiatrist in the world like a puppy licking your face."

Bernard Williams

Key Insights: *Explore the inner world of your puppy, including their dreams, emotions, interests, tail wagging, and body language.*

Have you ever been curious about what's going on in your puppy's mind? Wouldn't it be amazing if your puppy could clearly communicate their thoughts and feelings? While direct communication is beyond reach, you can gain a basic understanding of your puppy's psychology.

Delving into how your puppy thinks can help you interpret their actions and behaviors. Understanding the meaning behind a wagging tail, the nuances of their body language, and even their dreams can foster a deeper connection between you and your furry friend. This insight not only strengthens your bond but also enhances your ability to respond to their needs and emotions effectively.

Staring

When your puppy gazes at you with longing eyes, it's natural to wonder what's on their mind, especially if they've been fed and taken for a walk. Dogs often stare at their owners not out of boredom, but because they might want a treat, some playtime, or simply some affection. This intense focus can also be their way of seeking extra attention and love.

Looking Sad

Leaving your puppy alone while you go to work can make you feel guilty, especially if they seem sad. However, unless your puppy suffers from separation anxiety, they'll likely be just fine. Many puppies quickly adapt to their daily routines. They may appear confused or sad when you leave, but they usually adjust to your absence. It's helpful for them to understand the difference between your regular workday absence and a longer trip.

Barking Repeatedly

If your puppy barks persistently, especially at night, it might seem like they're just trying to disturb your sleep. However, dogs bark for specific reasons. They may be trying to get your attention, asking for a treat, wanting to go for a walk, or seeking to be released from confinement. Barking can also indicate that they sense something unusual or feel the need to alert you to potential danger. Since dogs often learn by repeating behaviors that get them what they want, consistent barking could mean they're used to getting a response from you.

Cocking Their Head

You've likely noticed your puppy tilting their head when you talk to them. This behavior isn't because they understand your story but rather serves multiple purposes. Your puppy might be trying to catch a familiar word, better understand what you're saying, or improve their ability to hear you. They may also be watching your facial expressions to gauge your message.

Understanding what goes on in your puppy's mind is an ongoing process. Over time, you'll become adept at interpreting their signals and understanding their needs with just a glance.

CHAPTER 3: BENEFITS OF CRATE TRAINING

""'I'll put her in charge of the puppies. I've twelve this week that need tending. How does that suit you?" Leeli's mouth hung open. She tried to say something but instead crumpled to the floor. She had fainted with joy."

Andrew Peterson, *The Monster in the Hollows*

Key Insight: *Crate training taps into puppies' natural denning instincts and offers numerous advantages.*

Using a crate offers many advantages for both you and your puppy. It provides a safe and secure space, which is particularly useful when transporting your pup to the vet, staying in a kennel, traveling to a hotel, or flying. Training your puppy to be comfortable in a crate can make these situations much less stressful. Let's explore the various benefits of crate training for you and your puppy.

Helps in Housebreaking

Puppies have a natural instinct to keep their living spaces clean, a trait inherited from their ancestors. This behavior can be leveraged to expedite housebreaking and prevent accidents in the house. When placed in a crate, puppies typically avoid soiling their sleeping area, holding off until they can go outside. By crating your puppy for short periods and then taking them to their designated toilet area, you encourage them to relieve themselves outdoors, rather than in the house.

Hinders Destructive Chewing

Puppies and even adult dogs often chew, especially during teething. To protect your belongings, it's crucial to teach them what is acceptable to chew. If allowed to chew on inappropriate items, this behavior can quickly become a habit. By supervising your puppy and redirecting their chewing to appropriate toys, you can guide them towards better behavior. When supervision isn't possible, placing your puppy in a crate with chew toys can prevent them from developing a habit of chewing on household items.

Keeps Your Dog Safe

If constant supervision is not feasible and there are many potential dangers or opportunities for mischief, crating your puppy can keep them safe. This prevents them from damaging your belongings or getting into dangerous situations.

Prevents the Formation of Problem Behaviors

Dogs naturally seek rewards and will repeat behaviors that yield positive outcomes. However, some of these behaviors, such as digging in the yard or getting into the trash, can be undesirable. By crating your puppy when you're not around, you can prevent them from engaging in these behaviors and forming bad habits. As your puppy matures, the amount of time they need to spend in the crate will decrease.

Safety and Security

A crate serves as a special sanctuary for your puppy, providing a place of peace, quiet, and comfort where they can relax and sleep. Much like a child's bedroom, a crate offers a sense of personal space and security for your dog, akin to their own little den.

Addressing Behavioral Problems

Combining training and management is key to resolving your puppy's behavioral issues. Training involves teaching your puppy to stop undesirable behaviors and encouraging good ones. Management means preventing opportunities for bad behavior. By crating your puppy when you can't supervise them, you can prevent them from engaging in unwanted activities and reinforce positive behavior.

Calming Your Puppy

A crate can be an effective tool for calming an overexcited puppy. If your puppy becomes too excited during play with other dogs or vigorous games, placing them in their crate can help them settle down and relax.

Safe Travel

For air travel, crating is essential for your puppy's safety and comfort. Familiarity with the crate can help them remain calm during the flight. While not always required in a car, crating your puppy during travel is advisable for safety reasons. It protects your puppy from potential injuries in case of an accident and prevents them from distracting the driver or attempting to climb out of the window.

CHAPTER 4: CRATE TRAINING BASICS

"As to which is cuter, a puppy or a baby, I'm going to say that probably depends less on the particular puppy and more on the baby. I've seen pictures of me as an infant and consider myself lucky that nobody ever offered my parents the opportunity to trade me for a beagle."

W. Bruce Cameron

Key Insight: Properly crate-trained puppies can travel safely and easily, with a personal space to retreat to. Crate training also aids in housebreaking and is a relatively quick process.

In the previous chapter, we discussed the various advantages of crate training. Now, let's dive into the essentials of getting started with crate training.

Introducing The Crate

Likely, your puppy hasn't spent much time in a crate, aside from travel or initial housebreaking by a breeder. Crate training will be a new experience for them. This training taps into your puppy's instinct to keep their living area clean, a trait inherited from their wild ancestors who would avoid soiling their den. Even though your puppy has never seen a real den, this instinct is still present.

Being in a crate triggers this natural behavior, encouraging them to avoid soiling their space. This makes crate training a useful tool for housebreaking. However, since your puppy views you as their pack, they may feel anxious when separated from you, which can lead to crying or whining in the crate. This isn't a dislike for the crate but rather a feeling of vulnerability. Your puppy is safe in the crate, but they need time to learn this.

Allow your puppy to become familiar with the crate, making it a comfortable space before expecting them to spend time inside. Never use the crate as a form of punishment; it should be a safe and positive space for your puppy. Here are some tips to help your puppy adjust to their new crate:

- **Keep the Door Open Initially:** Leave the crate door open and place treats inside to encourage your puppy to explore the crate on their own.
- **Feed in the Crate:** Feeding your puppy inside the crate can create a positive association between mealtime and the crate.
- **Make it Fun:** Incorporate games like hide and seek, where you hide a toy or treat in the crate and encourage your puppy to find it. Reward them with praise when they do.

Crate Training Safety

While crates are designed to keep your puppy safe, there are precautions you should take:

- **Avoid Chains and Slip Collars:** Never chain your puppy inside the crate or use slip collars, as these can get caught and cause panic or injury. Use a simple, undecorated collar.

- **Ensure Ventilation:** Make sure the crate is placed in a well-ventilated area. Avoid putting the crate in a hot room, under direct sunlight, or in a car on a hot day.
- **Supervise Children:** Ensure children do not tease the puppy by poking fingers through the crate or otherwise provoking them. This can make the puppy feel threatened and may lead to defensive behavior.

CHAPTER 5: HOW TO TEACH YOUR PUPPY ROUTINES

"Whenever I want to laugh, I read a wonderful book, 'Children's Letters to God.' You can open it anywhere. One I read recently said, 'Dear God, thank you for the baby brother, but what I prayed for was a puppy'."

Maya Angelou

Key Insight: Establishing a routine helps your puppy feel safe and secure by providing a sense of familiarity and structure. This routine also sets clear expectations for behavior.

Puppies are joyful little beings, but having a structured routine can be incredibly helpful for both training and providing a sense of security. A consistent schedule helps your puppy understand what is expected of them and when. Bringing a new puppy into your home is a significant adjustment for them, as it removes them from familiar surroundings and places them in a completely new environment.

Even the most confident puppies can feel anxious or scared in these circumstances. A routine helps provide familiarity, reducing surprises and easing the stress your puppy might experience. This consistency helps your puppy acclimate to their new home and understand the household rules and expectations.

House Rules

Before bringing your puppy home, it's important to establish clear rules that everyone in the household agrees on. Inconsistency can confuse your puppy; for example, if one person allows the puppy on the sofa while another scolds them for it, this mixed messaging can hinder their learning. Puppies thrive on consistency, so it's essential to decide in advance whether they are allowed on furniture, where they should sleep, and if they will have a crate. Once these rules are set, ensure that everyone in the home adheres to them.

Potty Routine

A consistent potty routine helps your puppy understand what's expected of them. Choose a convenient and easily cleanable location for potty training. It's crucial that everyone in the household knows this designated spot. Changing the location can confuse your puppy, so sticking to one area, marked by familiar smells, helps them understand where they should go.

Schedule regular potty breaks, ideally first thing in the morning, after lunch, in the evening, and right before bedtime. The frequency of these breaks will decrease as your puppy matures and gains better bladder control. In the early stages, frequent trips outside, especially after meals, can help prevent accidents inside the house.

Meal Schedule

Establish a set schedule for your puppy's meals and choose a specific location for feeding. Decide whether your puppy is allowed to have table scraps or not, and ensure everyone follows this rule. Inconsistent feeding practices, like sneaking table food to the puppy, can disrupt their training and encourage undesirable behaviors such as begging or stealing food.

If some family members want to give the puppy treats, consider placing these in the puppy's bowl after they finish their regular meal, or use them as rewards during training sessions. This approach maintains consistency in the puppy's diet and training.

Exercise Routine

A tired puppy is often a well-behaved puppy. Tailor your puppy's playtimes to match their energy levels and play style. Regular exercise is not only beneficial for your puppy's physical health, but it also helps expend their energy, leading to better behavior. Playtime is an excellent opportunity for bonding and reinforcing training. Use this time to practice basic obedience commands, spending a few minutes each day reviewing what your puppy has learned and introducing new commands.

CHAPTER 6: THE 5 ESSENTIAL COMMANDS TO TEACH YOUR PUPPY

"Disaster, to me, means in some big or small way, things going wrong. And that's obviously a matter of perception, right? Let's say your puppy chewed up all the shoes in your house. She probably had a fine time doing that. In her mind, a red letter day, the highlight of her puppy life."

Amy Gerstler

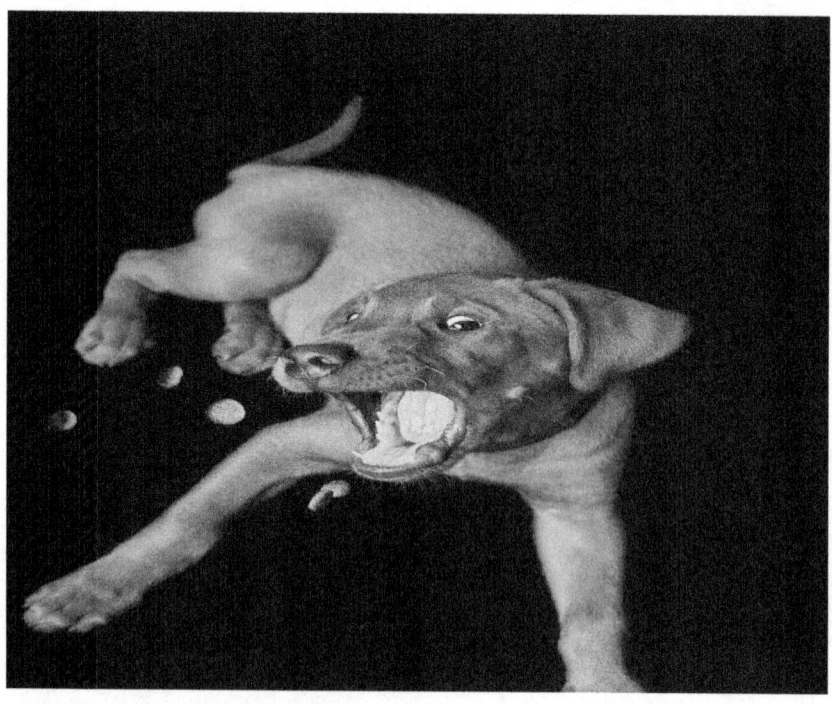

36 | *Welcome, adorable fluffball*

Key Insight: Commands are a way to communicate your expectations to your puppy, helping them understand what behaviors are desired or discouraged.

In this chapter, we will explore five fundamental commands that are crucial for training your puppy. These commands are:

- **Sit**
- **Stay**
- **Lie Down**
- **Recall (Come)**
- **Heel**

These basic commands are essential for effective communication with your puppy. Once these are mastered, you can move on to teaching more advanced commands.

Teaching Your Puppy to Sit

Begin by teaching your puppy to sit on command, which is a fundamental skill. When a puppy sits, it demonstrates politeness and a non-aggressive posture, indicating a readiness to wait. This command helps instill patience and attentiveness in your puppy.

To teach this command, stand calmly and assertively in front of your puppy. Make eye contact and say, "[your puppy's name], sit." Initially, hold a treat just above your puppy's nose, prompting them to raise their head and naturally lower their rear into a sitting position.

As soon as your puppy sits, reward them with praise and the treat. Say "Yes" or "Good Boy" to reinforce the positive behavior. The goal is for your puppy to associate the action with the reward and praise.

Gradually transition from using treats to hand signals. One common signal is placing the flat of your hand above your puppy's head and in front of their face while saying "Sit." Repeat this process consistently until your puppy reliably responds to the command.

Teaching the Command "Stay"

The "Stay" command is crucial for your puppy's safety, helping prevent them from entering dangerous situations. This command leverages a puppy's natural tendency to remain in place.

Start by having your puppy sit, then stand facing the same direction. This is known as the "place" stance. Gently hold your puppy's collar, say their name, followed by "Stay," and present your open palm towards them without touching. Your fingertips should point upwards.

Reward your puppy with a treat and praise if they stay in place. If they move, calmly reset and try again. Consistently repeat the command until your puppy understands to remain still.

Once your puppy grasps the concept, gradually extend the duration they are required to stay. If they get up prematurely, reset and try again. Introduce movement around your puppy while they stay in place, and use a release word like "okay" or "come" to signal they can move.

Teaching Your Puppy to Lie Down

Teaching your puppy to lie down is an important command, often used alongside "Stay" but with a stronger emphasis on controlling or calming your puppy. The "Down" command is useful for stopping undesirable behavior and ensuring your dog remains calm.

Begin with your puppy in a sitting position. Say your puppy's name followed by "Down." Hold your left hand above your puppy's head, palm facing down, while holding a treat in your right hand. Slowly lower your right hand towards the ground, guiding your puppy to follow the treat. As they follow the treat, they will naturally lower themselves into a lying position.

Once your puppy is lying down with elbows and hindquarters on the floor, praise them and reward them with the treat. This positive reinforcement helps your puppy associate the command with the action and the reward. Consistent repetition is key to mastering this command, ensuring your puppy understands and responds reliably.

Teaching Recall

Teaching your puppy to come when called, or "Recall," is essential for their safety and responsiveness. Start with your puppy in a sitting position, then gently encourage them to come to you by saying their name followed by "Come." Use an inviting tone and gesture with your hand to guide them.

You can also entice your puppy with a treat or a bit of dog food placed at your feet. When your puppy comes towards you, reward them with praise and a treat. Consistent positive reinforcement will help your puppy learn that coming to you is a good thing. Practice this command frequently in various situations to reinforce the behavior.

Teaching Your Dog to Heel

"Heel" is one of the more challenging commands to teach but is crucial for safe and enjoyable walks. It helps prevent your dog from pulling on the leash and ensures they stay close to you. Start by having your puppy sit beside you, both facing the same direction. Use your usual leash and have your puppy in the "sit" position at your left side, known as the "place" position.

Say your puppy's name followed by "Heel," and step forward with your left foot to indicate it's time to move. If your puppy tries to pull ahead or resist, gently tug on the leash and repeat the command. Encourage your puppy to stay close to you, using phrases like "Stay with me" or "Here." Be consistent and patient, rewarding your puppy with praise when they get it right.

If your puppy moves ahead, calmly say "Heel" and gently bring them back to your side. Practice stopping and having your puppy sit when you stop, reinforcing the behavior with verbal commands or hand signals.

Training Tips

When training your puppy, always maintain a calm and positive demeanor. Avoid showing frustration or irritation, as this can confuse or frighten your puppy, leading to a negative training experience. If you find yourself getting frustrated, take a break and resume training later.

Be firm yet gentle, and ensure your puppy understands that you are the leader. Consistency is key; don't delay or give up on training sessions. It's easier to start training a puppy than an older dog, so begin as early as possible.

Limit the number of people involved in training to avoid confusing your puppy with mixed signals. This helps create a clear and consistent learning environment, making it easier for your puppy to understand and follow commands.

CHAPTER 7: HOUSEBREAKING YOUR PUPPY IN 4 EASY STEPS

"I'm not alone," said the boy. "I've got a puppy."

Jane Thayer, *The Puppy Who Wanted a Boy*

Key Insight: Successful housebreaking is crucial for a harmonious relationship with your puppy. A housebroken puppy can enjoy more freedom within the home.

Housebreaking requires consistency, patience, and plenty of positive reinforcement. This process is about teaching your puppy good habits and strengthening your bond. The timeline for housebreaking can vary, typically taking

Welcome, adorable fluffball

between four to six months, though some puppies may take up to a year. The size of the puppy can influence this process; smaller puppies, with their smaller bladders and faster metabolisms, often need more frequent trips outside.

Additionally, your puppy's living conditions can impact housebreaking, as well as the need to eliminate any undesirable behaviors and reinforce positive ones. Establishing and maintaining a consistent schedule is essential for successful housebreaking.

Have Patience

Consistency and patience are key when housebreaking your puppy. Remember, your puppy doesn't understand human language and relies on your tone and body language for cues. It's normal to encounter setbacks during training, but these should not discourage you from continuing. If you notice your puppy showing signs of needing to go outside, promptly take them out and reward them for going in the right place. This positive reinforcement helps them learn what is expected.

When to Start Housebreaking

Housebreaking should ideally begin when the puppy is 12 to 16 weeks old, as they can better control their bladder and bowel movements at this age. Starting later may prolong the training process, especially if the puppy has developed the habit of eliminating in their crate. Consistent encouragement and rewards are crucial in helping them learn new, desirable behaviors.

Confining your puppy's space can aid in housebreaking, as puppies generally avoid soiling the areas where they sleep and eat. This method encourages them to seek a designated spot outside for their needs.

Create a Schedule

Establish a consistent feeding and potty schedule for your puppy. Do not leave food in their bowl between meals. Take your puppy outside immediately after they wake up, after meals, after naps, and after playtime. Regular potty breaks, ideally every hour, are essential, especially before bedtime.

Take your puppy to the same spot each time, as the familiar scent will encourage them to go. Stay outside with your puppy until they have finished. Always reward them with praise or a treat when they do their business outside; even a walk can serve as a reward.

Using a Crate

A crate can be an effective tool in housebreaking, but it should not be used for more than two hours at a time, except overnight. The crate should be appropriately sized—not too big, to avoid the puppy using part of it as a bathroom, and not too small, to ensure comfort. If you're unable to stay with your puppy during the day, arrange for someone to take them for walks. If your puppy starts using the crate as a bathroom, stop using it for training purposes.

Common signs that your puppy needs to go out include sniffing the ground, barking, whining, circling, or scratching at the door. Accidents will happen during training; handle them calmly and clean the area thoroughly. If you catch your puppy about to go inside, firmly but gently say "no" and immediately take them outside.

CHAPTER 8: HOW TO CORRECT BAD BEHAVIOR

"Puppies are constantly inventing new ways to be bad. It's fascinating. You come into a room they've been in and see pieces of debris and try to figure out what you had that was made from wicker or what had been stuffed with fluff."

Julie Klam, *You Had Me at Woof: How Dogs Taught Me the Secrets of Happiness*

Key Insight: It's crucial to address and correct bad behavior in puppies. They are energetic and curious, so it's important to teach them what behaviors are acceptable and which are not.

Bringing home a cute, cuddly puppy often comes with unexpected challenges, as they can quickly become little troublemakers. It's important to teach your puppy what behaviors are acceptable. Before tackling bad behavior, it helps if your puppy has already learned basic commands like sit, stay, come, and down. These commands form the foundation for further training and behavior correction.

Dogs Need Rules

Consistency is crucial in a dog's life. Establishing a few basic rules that everyone in the household follows is important for effective training. Regardless of age, a dog will act as it pleases if not properly trained. When correcting your dog's behavior, always remain calm and composed. Avoid yelling, screaming, shouting, or hitting, as these actions can create fear rather than respect.

Training Your Puppy

Basic obedience training is essential for correcting unwanted behaviors. Your puppy should learn basic verbal or hand commands, ideally starting around three or four months old. This training includes commands like sit, stay, come, and down, as discussed in previous chapters. Puppies can be enrolled in obedience classes as early as 10 weeks old, which also helps them socialize with other dogs.

Common behavior issues include:

- Biting/Chewing
- Jumping on people
- Playing rough
- Begging
- Excessive barking
- Digging

Let's explore how to address these issues.

Stop Your Dog From Biting and Chewing

Puppies naturally use their mouths when playing, often mimicking behaviors from interactions with their littermates. This can include nipping, which is a dog's way of communicating or setting boundaries. However, it's important to discourage biting or mouthing, especially since puppies have sharp teeth.

If your puppy bites during play, let out a small yelp and say "ouch" to startle them and stop the behavior. Immediately praise and reward your puppy when they stop. If they bite your hand, let out a loud yelp but do not pull away, which encourages them to release. Offer them a chew toy as a positive alternative. Providing appropriate chew toys is essential, especially during teething, to prevent damage to household items like shoes and furniture.

Stop Jumping

Dogs often jump on people when they are excited, whether when greeting someone at the door or meeting new people. To curb this behavior, use the "Off" command. One effective training method involves having a friend or family member enter the home while your dog is on a leash. When your dog attempts to jump, gently tug on the leash and firmly say "Off," followed by "Sit." Once your dog is sitting calmly, praise and reward them.

Alternatively, you can ignore your dog completely when they jump, avoiding eye contact until they settle down. Once calm, offer praise and affection, reinforcing the behavior you want to see.

Stopping Rough Play

When your dog starts to play too roughly, it can quickly escalate into a potentially dangerous situation. It's important not to encourage your dog to grab or attack any part of your body, as this can lead to injuries, especially as they grow older and stronger. If your dog gets too rough during a game like tug of war, use the command "drop it" to signal them to release the toy. If this doesn't work, say the command again, then get up and walk away. This teaches your dog that rough play will end the game.

Stopping Begging

If your dog often begs for food while you're eating, it's likely because they've been given food from the table in the past, reinforcing this behavior. To discourage begging, feed your dog at the same time you eat, but in a different location. You can place them in their crate or another room during mealtimes. When your dog begs, firmly tell them "no" and redirect them to sit and stay. Consistency is key in breaking this habit, so be patient and persistent.

Managing Excessive Barking

Teaching your dog the "speak" and "quiet" commands can help manage excessive barking. Start by encouraging your dog to bark on command using the word "speak," rewarding them with a treat when they comply. Once your dog understands "speak," introduce the "quiet" command. Get your dog to bark, then say "quiet" and hold back the treat until they stop barking. Reward them when they are quiet to reinforce the behavior.

Addressing Digging

Digging is a natural behavior for dogs, often used to cool down or bury items. To curb this behavior, provide your dog with plenty of exercise to tire them out and reduce the urge to dig. You can also limit their access to certain areas of the yard or supervise them closely. If your dog starts digging, gently discourage the behavior.

To further deter digging, consider placing chicken wire over the area they are digging. The uncomfortable sensation can discourage them from continuing. Alternatively, filling the holes with their own feces and covering them with soil can be effective, as dogs generally avoid the scent of their waste. If possible, designate a specific area in the yard where digging is allowed, and train your dog to use only that area.

Seeking Professional Help

If you're struggling to correct your dog's behavior, professional help may be beneficial. Consult with your veterinarian to rule out any medical issues that might be influencing your dog's behavior. Your vet can also recommend professional dog trainers who can provide additional guidance and support.

Welcome, adorable fluffball

CHAPTER 9: FINAL TIPS FOR TRAINING YOUR PUPPY

"I love words. Sudoku I don't get into, I'm not into numbers that much, and there are people who are hooked on that. But crossword puzzles, I just can't - if I get a puppy and I paper train him and I put the - if all of a sudden I'd open the paper and there's a crossword puzzle - 'No, no, you can't go on that, honey. I'll take it'."

Betty White

Welcome, adorable fluffball

Key Insight: Training your puppy begins when they are old enough. Whether you choose to train them yourself or seek professional assistance, there are key strategies to keep in mind: be affectionate, patient, consistent, and attentive to your puppy's needs.

In this chapter, we'll explore essential tips to consider during the training process.

Listen to Your Puppy

It's important to pay attention to your puppy's signals. If they seem uneasy around another dog, animal, or person, don't force them into the situation. Your puppy is communicating discomfort, and it's crucial to respect their boundaries. Pushing them to interact when they're not ready can lead to behavioral problems later on.

Show Plenty of Affection

While it's easy to show disapproval when your puppy misbehaves, don't forget to acknowledge the good behavior too. This is a common oversight. Make sure to give your puppy plenty of praise, affection, and attention when they do something right. Positive reinforcement helps them understand that they are behaving well and encourages them to repeat those behaviors. Be generous with your affection to reinforce positive actions.

Consider Your Puppy's Preferences

Not all treats labeled "dog treats" will be appealing to your puppy. Just like humans, dogs have their own tastes and preferences. Observe what your puppy genuinely enjoys and use those treats as rewards during training. This not only makes training more effective but also more enjoyable for your puppy.

Give Clear Instructions

While using the "no" command can stop unwanted behavior, it doesn't provide your puppy with guidance on what to do instead. Dogs don't naturally understand general instructions; they need specific directions. For example, if your puppy jumps on someone, saying "no" may just confuse them, possibly leading them to jump differently. Instead, instruct your puppy to "sit," giving them a clear and positive action to focus on.

Maintain Consistency

Consistency is crucial in training your puppy. All family members must agree on the rules and use the same commands. Inconsistent commands or allowances will confuse your puppy, making it harder for them to learn. For example, if one person uses "off" to mean get off the couch and another uses "down," this inconsistency can be confusing for the puppy. Everyone should use the same terms and follow the same rules.

Set Realistic Expectations

Behavioral changes take time, especially if your puppy has been engaging in certain behaviors for a long period. Common behaviors like barking, digging, or jumping to greet people require patience and consistent effort to change. It's important to recognize that these behaviors won't disappear overnight, and consistent reinforcement of new, desirable behaviors is key.

Provide a Proper Diet

Your puppy's diet is essential for their health and behavior. The diet should be appropriate for the level of activity your dog engages in. For instance, a working dog requires more protein than a mostly sedentary dog. While high-protein diets are generally beneficial, it's important to ensure your puppy is primarily eating dog food rather than human food. Consult with your veterinarian to establish a balanced diet that supports your puppy's overall well-being.

Use Reinforcement Wisely

If your puppy exhibits behaviors you don't like, it's possible these behaviors have been inadvertently reinforced. For instance, if your dog brings a toy and barks until you throw it, and you comply, the dog learns that barking achieves their goal. Instead of giving in, redirect the behavior by instructing your puppy to "sit" or "stay quiet." Reinforce the behaviors you want to encourage rather than those you wish to discourage.

Bribery Doesn't Work

Avoid using treats to bribe your dog into doing something. Treats should be used as rewards, not as a form of bribery. When treats are used as bribes, you give your dog the power to decide whether to comply based on the reward offered. Training sessions should be about learning and following commands, not about making choices based on treats. Your dog should want to follow your commands out of respect and training, not just for treats.

Granting Freedom Gradually

Your dog should earn its freedom in the house gradually. Many pet owners make the mistake of giving their dog too much freedom too quickly, which can lead to housebreaking accidents and the development of destructive behaviors. Use baby gates to restrict access to unoccupied rooms, ensuring your dog is safe and supervised.

The safest way to monitor your dog is by keeping them close to you, especially during the initial stages of training. Start by showing your dog safe areas and gradually increase their freedom as they demonstrate good behavior and understanding of household rules. This controlled approach helps prevent accidents and reinforces positive behavior patterns.

CHAPTER 10: NEXT-LEVEL TRAINING

In previous chapters, we've covered the basics of training your puppy, including fundamental commands, housebreaking, and managing behavior. Now, it's time to delve into more advanced training techniques that will not only enhance your puppy's skills but also strengthen the bond between you and your furry friend.

Key Insight: Advanced training builds on basic skills, promoting better communication, mental stimulation, and socialization for your puppy.

Building on Basic Commands

Now that your puppy has mastered basic commands like sit, stay, come, and down, it's time to introduce more complex commands and behaviors.

Off-Leash Training

Start practicing commands without a leash, in a safe and enclosed area. Off-leash training enhances your dog's reliability and responsiveness. Begin with short distances, gradually increasing as your puppy becomes more confident. Always reward your puppy for responding correctly, reinforcing their good behavior.

Distance Commands

Teach your puppy to obey commands from a distance. Start with simple commands like "sit" and "stay," then increase the distance between you and your puppy. Use clear hand signals to communicate with your dog, which is especially useful when verbal commands are less effective in noisy environments.

Advanced Tricks and Skills

Teaching your puppy new tricks and skills can be a fun and rewarding way to provide mental stimulation.

Fetch and Retrieve

Enhance the basic fetch game by teaching your dog to retrieve specific items by name. Start by naming a favorite toy and encouraging your dog to fetch it. Gradually introduce other items, rewarding your puppy for retrieving the correct one.

Target Training

Target training involves teaching your dog to touch a specific target, like your hand or a stick, with their nose or paw. This can be useful for guiding your dog into specific positions or behaviors and can be a precursor to more complex tasks like closing doors or turning off lights.

Impulse Control and Focus

Impulse control and focus are critical for a well-behaved dog, especially in distracting environments.

Leave It and Take It

These commands teach your puppy to resist the temptation of grabbing items they shouldn't. "Leave it" instructs your dog to ignore an object, while "Take it" gives permission to engage with it. Start with less tempting items and gradually introduce more tempting ones, rewarding your puppy for following the command.

Eye Contact

Training your puppy to maintain eye contact can improve focus and strengthen your bond. Begin by holding a treat near your face and rewarding your puppy when they make eye contact. Gradually increase the duration of eye contact before giving the treat.

Socialization and Public Etiquette

Advanced training also includes socialization and proper behavior in public spaces.

Calmness Around Other Dogs and People

Teach your puppy to remain calm around other dogs and people. Practice in controlled environments, gradually exposing your dog to busier areas. Use commands like "sit" or "stay" to manage your puppy's behavior, rewarding calm and polite interactions.

Manners in Public Places

Train your puppy to behave well in public places, such as cafes, parks, and pet-friendly stores. This includes not jumping on people, not begging for food, and staying calm in crowded or noisy environments. Practice these skills regularly, rewarding good behavior and providing guidance as needed.

Continued Learning and Challenges

Advanced training is an ongoing process that keeps your dog's mind sharp and engaged.

Agility Training

Agility training is a great way to challenge your dog's physical and mental abilities. Start with simple obstacles like tunnels and jumps, gradually increasing the complexity. This not only provides exercise but also improves your dog's coordination and focus.

Problem-Solving Games

Introduce your puppy to puzzle toys and games that require problem-solving skills. These activities can help prevent boredom and keep your puppy mentally stimulated, which is essential for overall well-being.

CONCLUSION

Bringing a puppy into your home is an incredibly joyous experience. Those big, innocent eyes can melt anyone's heart, even after a mischievous escapade in the kitchen. But with the right training, you can have a well-behaved dog and still enjoy the playful nature of a puppy.

This guide, *Puppy Training Techniques*, has equipped you with the knowledge and tools to train your puppy effectively. You've learned:

- The five essential commands: "Sit," "Stay," "Lie Down," "Recall," and "Heel"
- How to interpret your puppy's body language

- The benefits of crate training
- Effective housebreaking strategies
- How to address and correct unwanted behaviors like biting, jumping, and excessive barking

Training a puppy requires time, effort, and patience, but the rewards are well worth it. Start with basic commands to build a foundation, then introduce crate training. Begin respect and acceptance training early on. Housebreaking can take time, so start as soon as possible. Once your puppy has mastered these basics, you can move on to more advanced tricks and skills. Always be patient and consistent, and never lose sight of the importance of training.

Throughout this process, you're also building a strong bond with your puppy. By setting boundaries with love and care, your puppy learns not only what is acceptable but also that you are a trusted guide. This trust and understanding will strengthen your relationship, bringing joy and companionship to both of you.

Wishing you and your puppy the very best as you embark on this journey together. Enjoy every moment of the training and the fun that comes with it

BONUS

HOW TO CHOOSE YOUR PUPPY

Choosing the right puppy is a significant decision that requires careful thought and consideration. Here's a detailed guide to help you make an informed choice:

1. Assess Your Lifestyle

- **Activity Level:** Consider how active you are and how much time you can dedicate to exercising a dog. High-energy breeds require regular exercise, while more sedentary breeds may be better suited for less active owners.
- **Living Situation:** Your home environment plays a crucial role. Larger breeds need more space, while smaller breeds may be comfortable in apartments.
- **Time Commitment:** Puppies require significant time for training, socialization, and care. Evaluate

your daily schedule to ensure you can meet these needs.

2. Research Breeds

- **Size and Lifespan:** Breeds vary in size, from small lap dogs to large working breeds. Consider the space available in your home and the breed's typical lifespan.
- **Temperament:** Each breed has a distinct personality. Some are more independent, while others crave constant companionship. Choose a breed that aligns with your expectations.
- **Health and Grooming:** Some breeds are prone to specific health issues. Research common problems and ensure you're prepared for potential medical costs. Grooming needs also vary; some breeds require regular professional grooming, while others are low-maintenance.

3. Consider the Source

- **Adoption vs. Breeder:** Adoption is a compassionate choice that provides a home to a dog in need. Reputable breeders can offer puppies with known backgrounds and health guarantees. If adopting, look for shelters and rescue groups with good reputations. If buying from a breeder, ensure they follow ethical breeding practices and prioritize the health and well-being of their dogs.

4. Visit and Observe

- **First Impressions:** Spend time observing the puppies' behavior. Look for signs of a healthy puppy: clear eyes, clean ears, a shiny coat, and a playful demeanor. Notice if the puppy is curious, friendly, and comfortable being handled.
- **Temperament Testing:** Observe how the puppy interacts with its littermates and people. Is it more dominant or submissive? Does it seem shy or outgoing? These behaviors can give you a glimpse into the puppy's future temperament.

5. Ask Questions

- **Health and Background:** Whether adopting or buying, ask about the puppy's health records, vaccination history, and any known genetic issues. Inquire about the parents' health and temperament, as these can influence the puppy's future behavior and health.
- **Breeder Practices:** If purchasing from a breeder, ask about their breeding practices. A responsible breeder should provide proof of health clearances

for the parents, offer a health guarantee for the puppy, and be willing to answer all your questions.

6. Trust Your Instincts

- **Connection and Comfort:** Choose a puppy that you feel a connection with. A good fit means that the puppy's energy levels, temperament, and needs align with your lifestyle and capabilities.
- **Future Considerations:** Remember, this decision is for the long term. Consider how your life might change in the next 10-15 years and whether you can commit to the puppy's care throughout its life.

Choosing a puppy is a joyful and rewarding experience. By taking the time to make an informed decision, you'll lay the foundation for a happy and fulfilling relationship with your new furry friend.

Printed in Great Britain
by Amazon